Clip Art Assembly Basics

Here are some suggestions as you make your flyers, announce(
from this book.

Tools

Putting together the right tools for the project will make it go smoother and look better in the end. A good **copy machine** is a must. It's worth the extra effort to make sure your school or copy shop has machines that make clean copies. You will also need a bottle of white **paper correction fluid**, a fine-tip **black marker** to combine the designs and add your own art to the project, **rubber cement** to mount the design onto your paper during the layout stage of your project, and **scissors** for cutting apart the designs you choose. Optional tools to help create a professional-looking project are a **non-reproducible blue pencil**, to make marks that will not show up on copies; a **proportion scale**, to help you determine the size of the reduction or enlargement necessary to fit your paper; and **blue grid paper** for laying out the project with straight lines.

Assembly Steps

1. Choose the design or designs you will be putting together for the project that you will be making.

2. Copy the design once from the book so that you have a copy from which to work without having to cut apart your book.

3. Cut out the designs from your copy and lay them out on your paper. (Blue grid paper comes in handy.) A light table can also help with the layout of your page.

4. Next, make a copy of the designs and any text on the paper before adding any other hand-drawn illustrations. Drawing over the grid paper lines is difficult and generally doesn't turn out well.

5. Now you have a good idea of what your project is going to look like. Go ahead and add all the extra finishing touches. Small doodles drawn on each page of **Colossal Clip Art** will give you some ideas of possible additions. Even simple dots or squares can really "warm up" the page and keep it from looking choppy.

6. Make your final copies of the page. Easy!

Hints

• Keep a ¼ inch margin on all edges of your paper.

• If the edges of the cut-out pieces are visible on your copies, lighten the copy machine one notch or use correction fluid on one copy and then use it to make final copies.

• Removable tape is great for creating layouts if you will be using the design more than once.

Have fun with your projects! You can become an artist and create wonderful projects for your class with the help of this book!

3

5

7

11

13

FALL ASSEMBLY SCHEDULE

To the Parents of _____

FALL PROGRESS REPORT

21

SCHOOL ANNOUNCEMENTS

SEPTEMBER

FALL HALL PASS

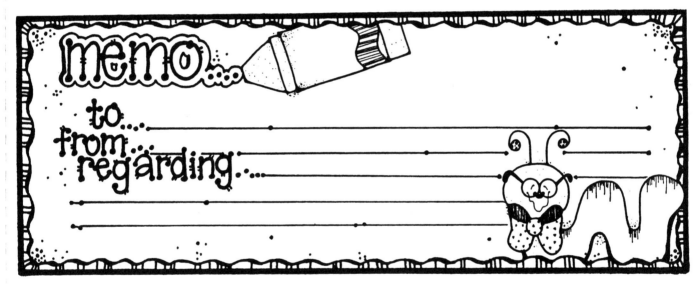

memo...

to..._____
from..._____
regarding..._____
_____
_____

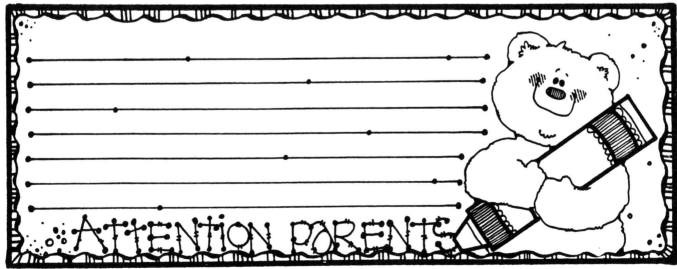

_____
_____
_____
_____
_____
_____

ATTENTION PARENTS

a note to volunteers...

SUBSTITUTE SCHEDULE

TEACHER:
ROOM #:
COMMENTS:
DATE:

FROM THE DESK OF...

READING

MATH

OTHER

SPELLING

SOCIAL STUDIES / SCIENCE

DINOMITE SCHOOL!

33

You're DINOMITE!

41

43

47

GO TEAM GO!

51

SCHOOL ANNOUNCEMENTS OCTOBER

HAPPY HALLOWEEN

59

63

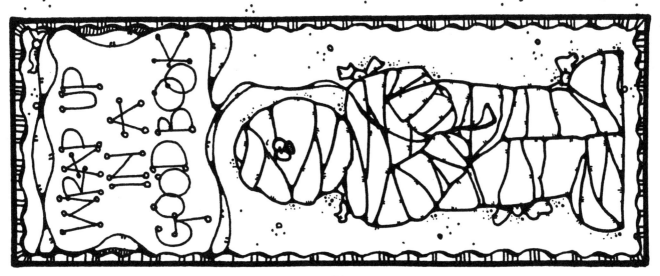

HaLLoWeeN party !!

WISE OL' OWL...

71

75

79

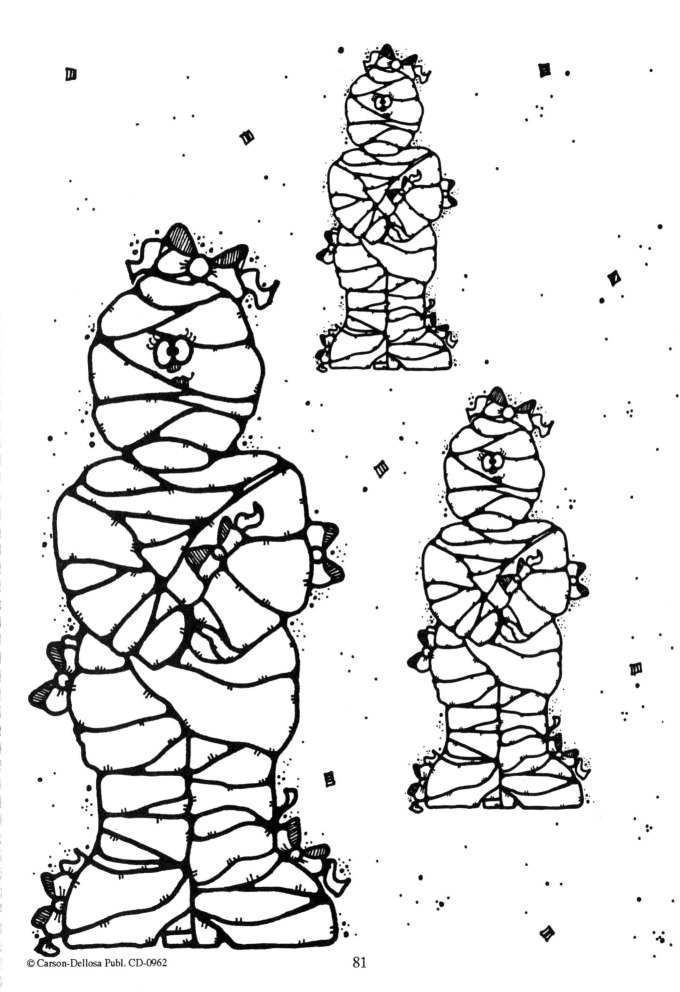

81

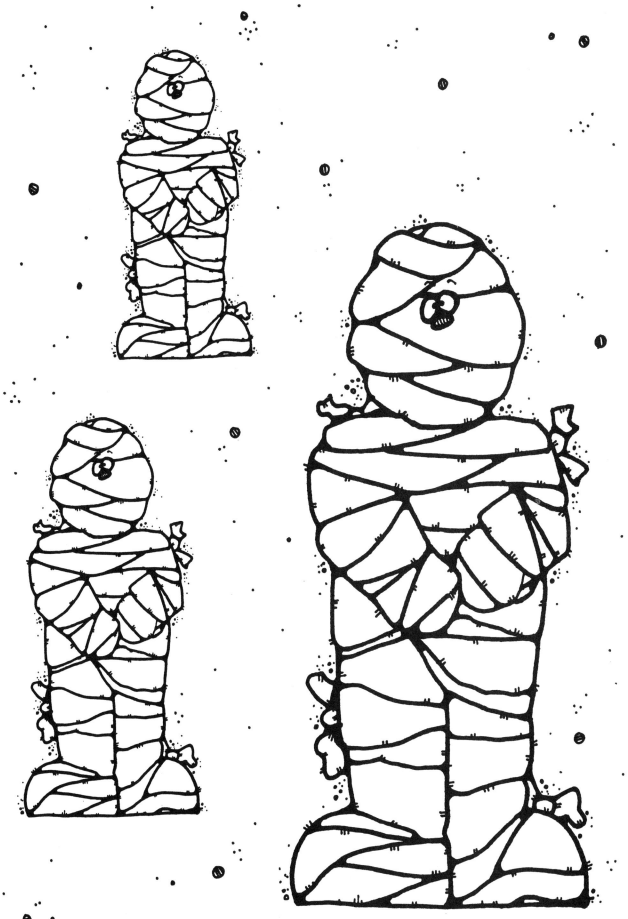

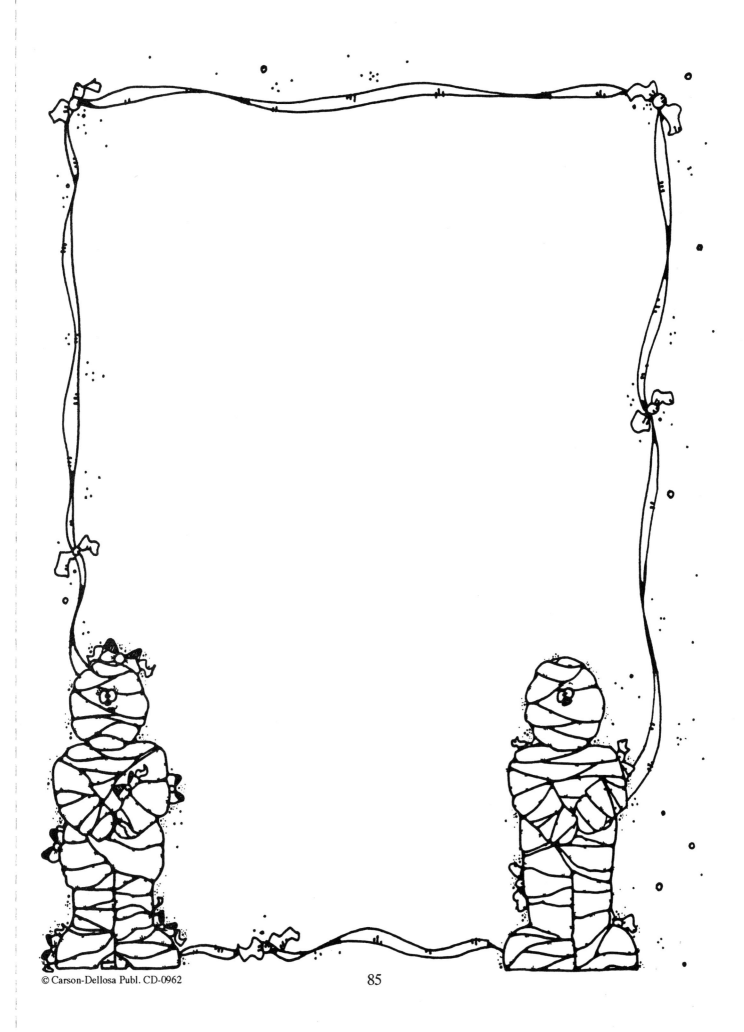

91

...·October·...

STUDENT OF THE MONTH
AWARDED TO...

NAME

TEACHER   DATE

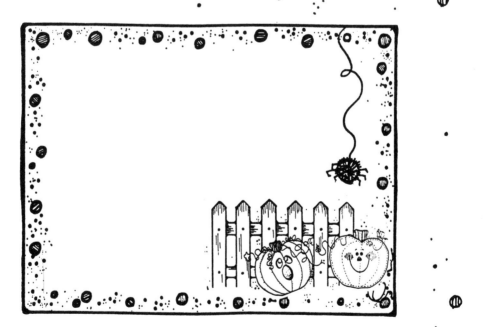

95

97

SCHOOL ANNOUNCEMENTS
NOVEMBER

99

turkey day!

SOMETHING SUPER TO EAT...

Turkey Time Treats...

A RECIPE FOR...

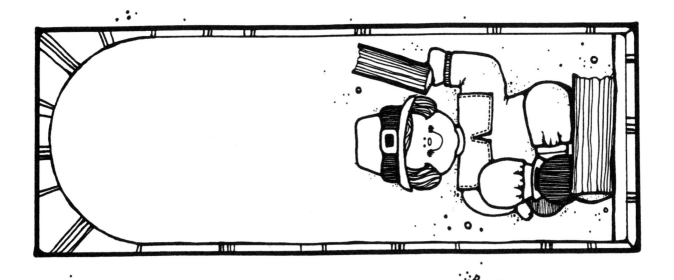

111

YUMMY

115

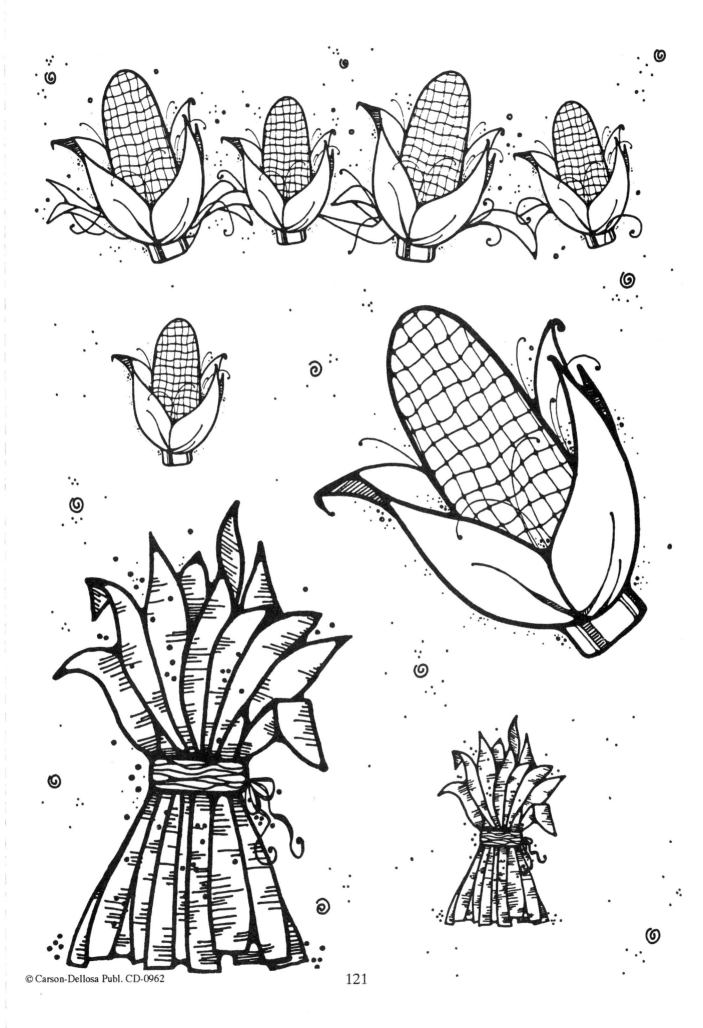

121

I'm Thankful for...

···November···

STUDENT OF THE MONTH
AWARDED TO

_____

NAME

_____

_____

_____   _____

TEACHER   DATE

THIS
BELONGS
TO:

HOMEWORK

Please sign and return

131

READ

READ

133

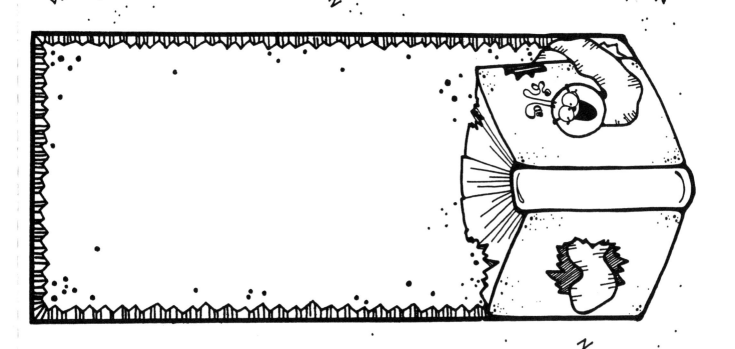

135

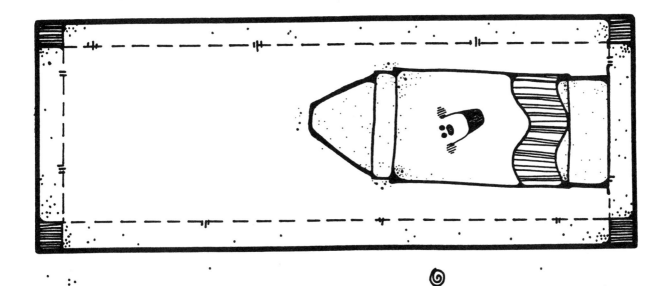

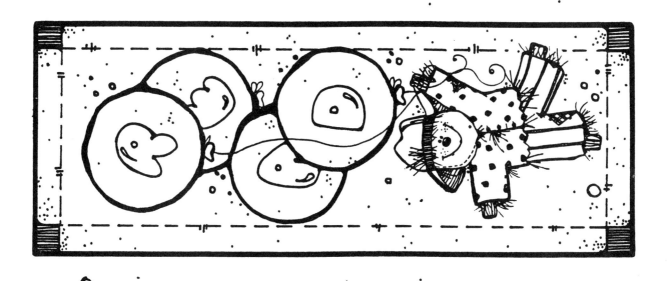

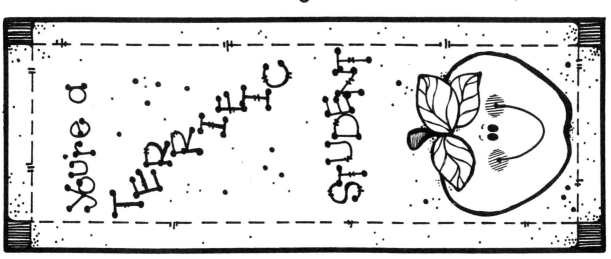

You're a TERRIFIC STUDENT

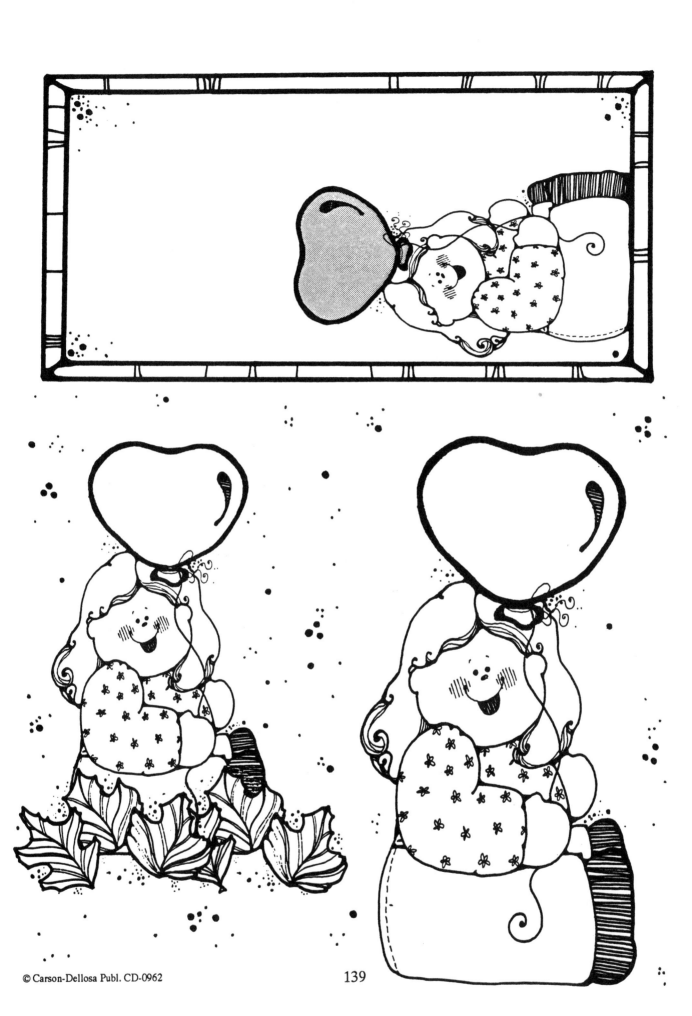

READING ASSIGNMENT

BOOK CLUB!

try harder !

Nice Job !

GOOD WORK

Terrific

Well Done!

GREAT WOW!

LIBRARY

LIBRARY

Your books are overdue!

MATH HOMEWORK

149

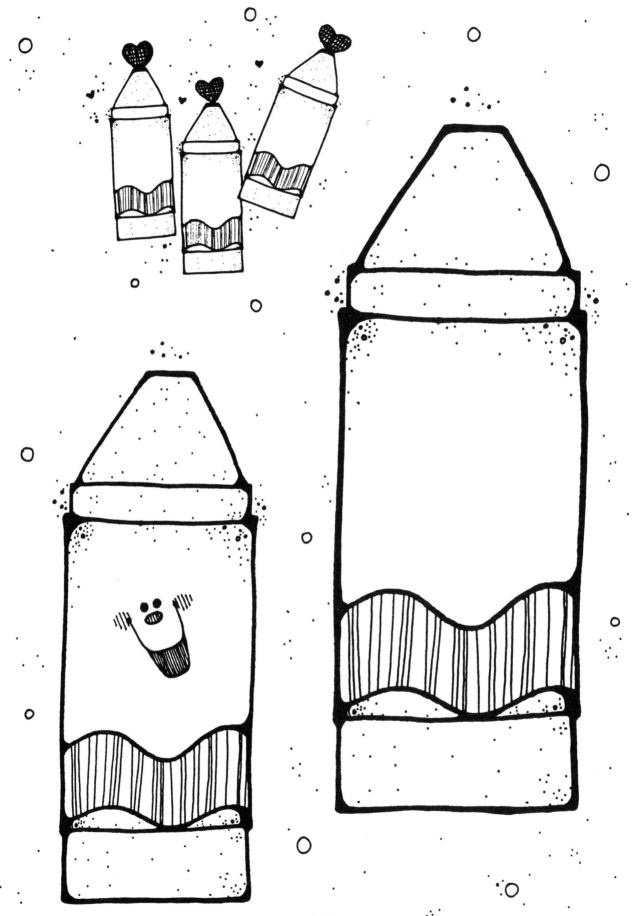

153

YOU REALLY MEASURE UP!

157

159

Please help your child with the homework listed below...

_____

_____

_____

_____

_____

_____

161

got caught being good

name

date   teacher

got caught being good

name

date   teacher

got caught being good

name

date   teacher

SPELLING
BEE

SUPER SPELLER

SPELLING BEE

SUPER SPELLER !!

awarded to

teacher

date

"HIP·HIPPO·RAY" FOR YOU!!

_____ name

_____ date

_____ teacher

171

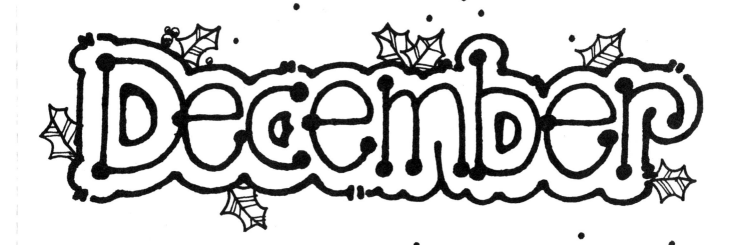

February

173

DECEMBER ANNOUNCEMENTS

175

CHRISTMAS PLAY

Date ...
Time ...

177

Dear Santa...

A Reminder to our volunteers...

❄ ...fold note on lines indicated and insert tab in slot...

fold

fold

From:

To:

fold

fold

185

fold

fold

Happy Holidays from your Teacher

187

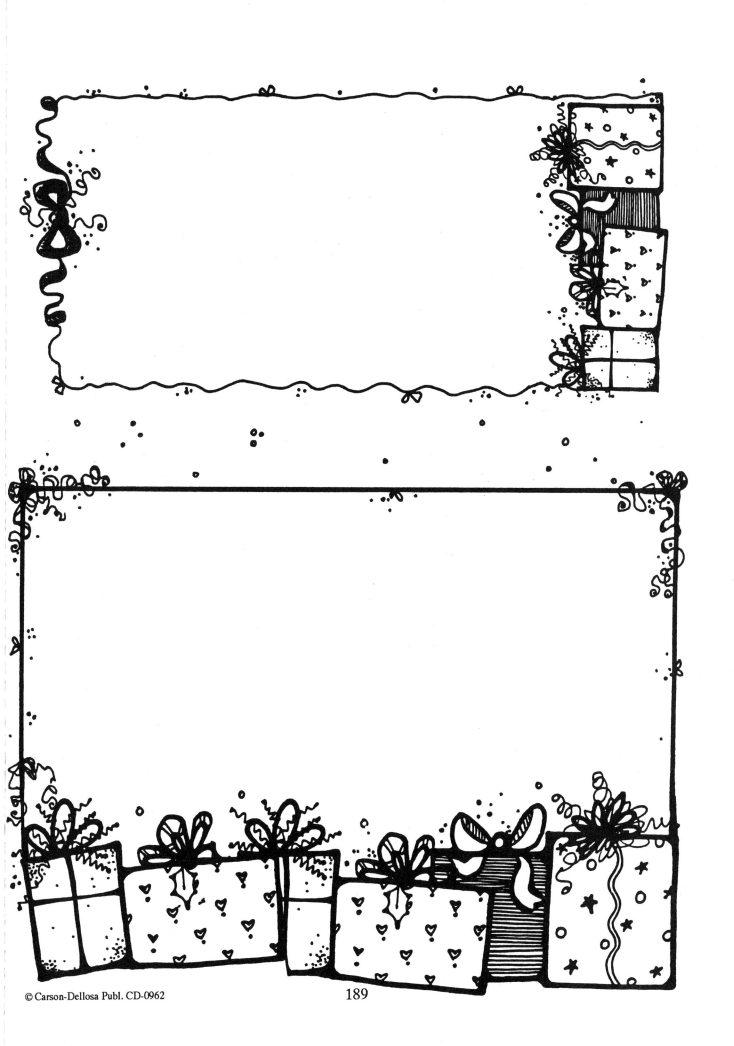

191

you're an angel !

193

195

MERRY-CHRISTMAS

Happy Holidays!

HO HO HO

WINTER

Hanukkah

season's
Greetings

BAH
HUMBUG

Happy Holidays!

MERRY CHRISTMAS

Great Work!

Happy Holidays

205

207

209

211

213

To...

From...

Merry Christmas

Happy Holidays

to:

from:

To...

From...

Just a little treat!

to..

from..

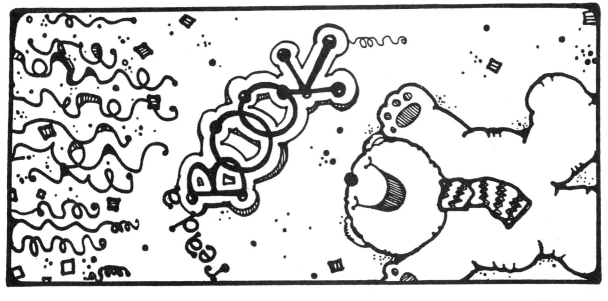

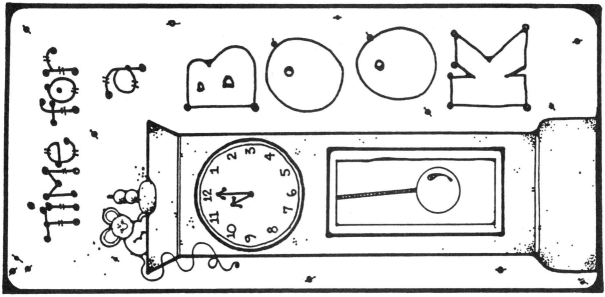

PERFECT WORK

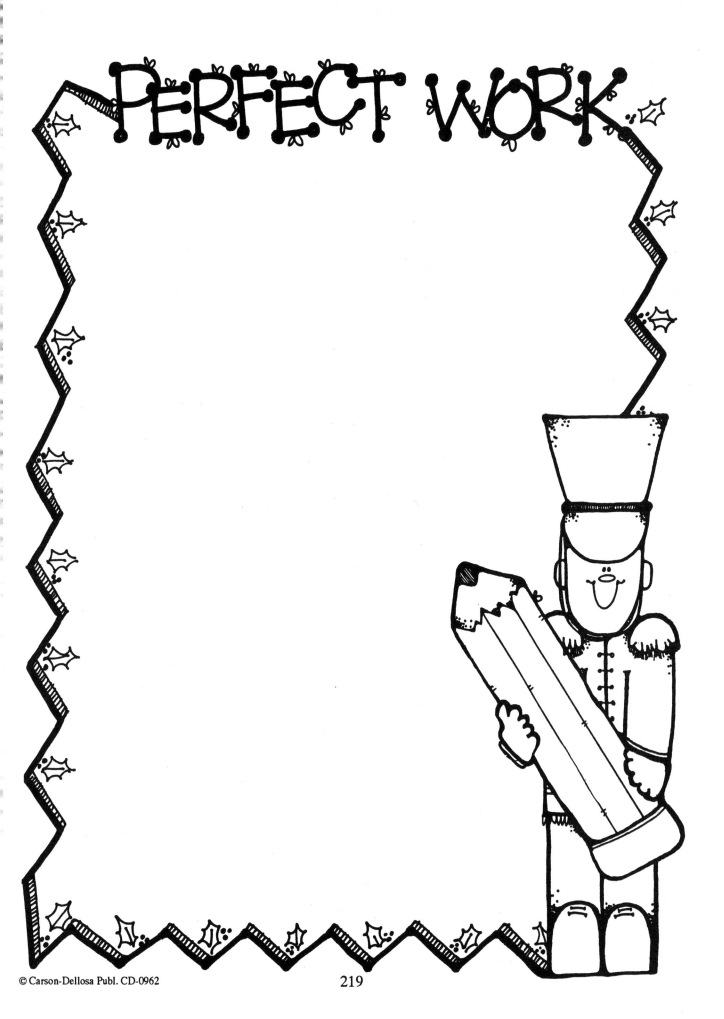

DECEMBER

Student of the Month

_____ to _____

_____ for

_____

date   teacher

JANUARY ANNOUNCEMENTS

229

Keep up the good work

TO: _____

From: _____

BIG IMPROVEMENT

TO: _____

For: _____

YOU DID IT!

To: _____

For: _____

243

245

THANK YOU

from your teacher!

fold

fold

THIS BELONGS TO

_____
name

_____
grade

_____
teacher

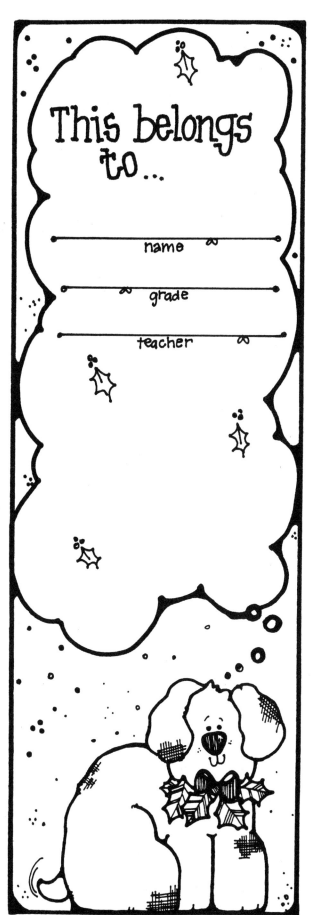

This belongs to...

_____
name

_____
grade

_____
teacher

JANUARY

Student of the Month

to _____

_____
for

_____
date   teacher

FEBRUARY ANNOUNCEMENTS

Valentine Notes

Valentine wishes from your Teacher

To:

HAPPY VALENTINES DAY

TO:

FROM:

You're "SSSuper" Valentine!

To:

From:

A Special Valentine

To:

From:

263

Happy Valentine's Day!

AWESOME!

269

FANTASTIC!

273

VALENTINE PARTY!

279

THiS iS DiNOMiTE STUFF...

GREAT BEHAVIOR
AWARD!

to

for

from

date

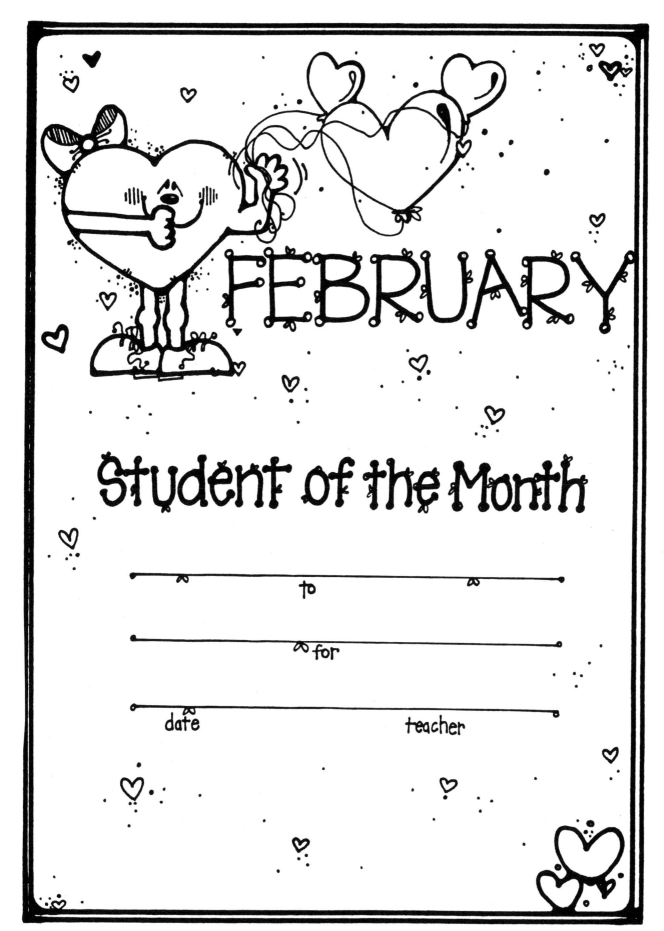

FEBRUARY

Student of the Month

_____ to _____

_____ for _____

date   teacher

BASKETBALL

PRACTICE SCHEDULE

293

SPELLING LIST

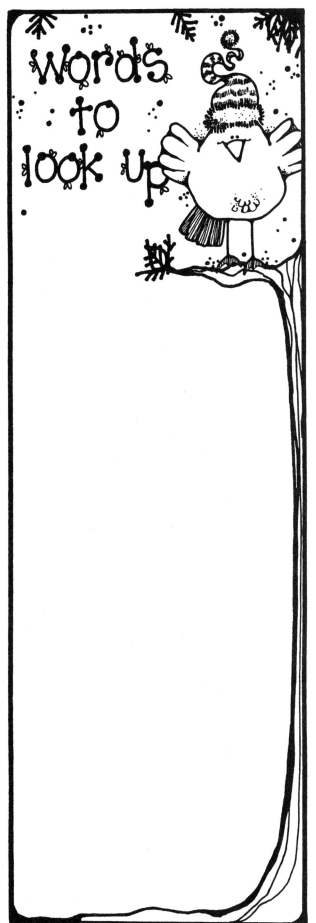

words to look up

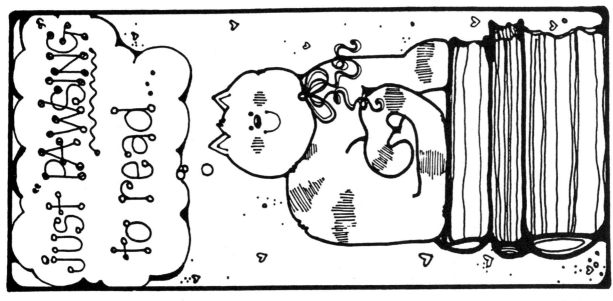

Just PAWSING to read ...

JUMP into a good book!

THiS BOOK iS DOG-GONE GREAT!

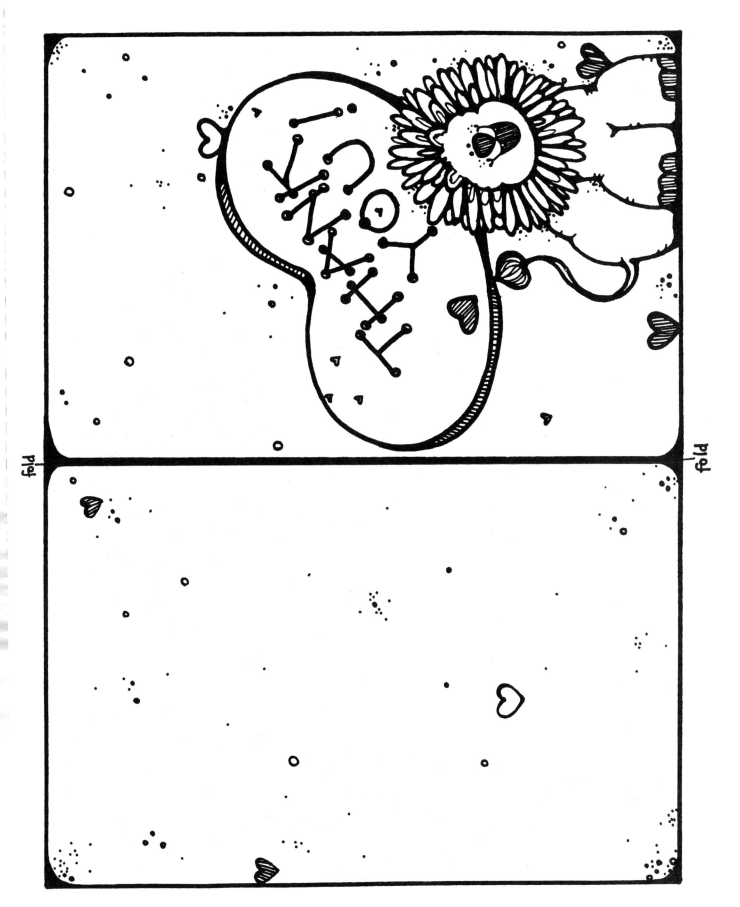

OFFICE PASS

HALL PASS

303

WONDERFUL WORK !

307

A note to our Volunteers...

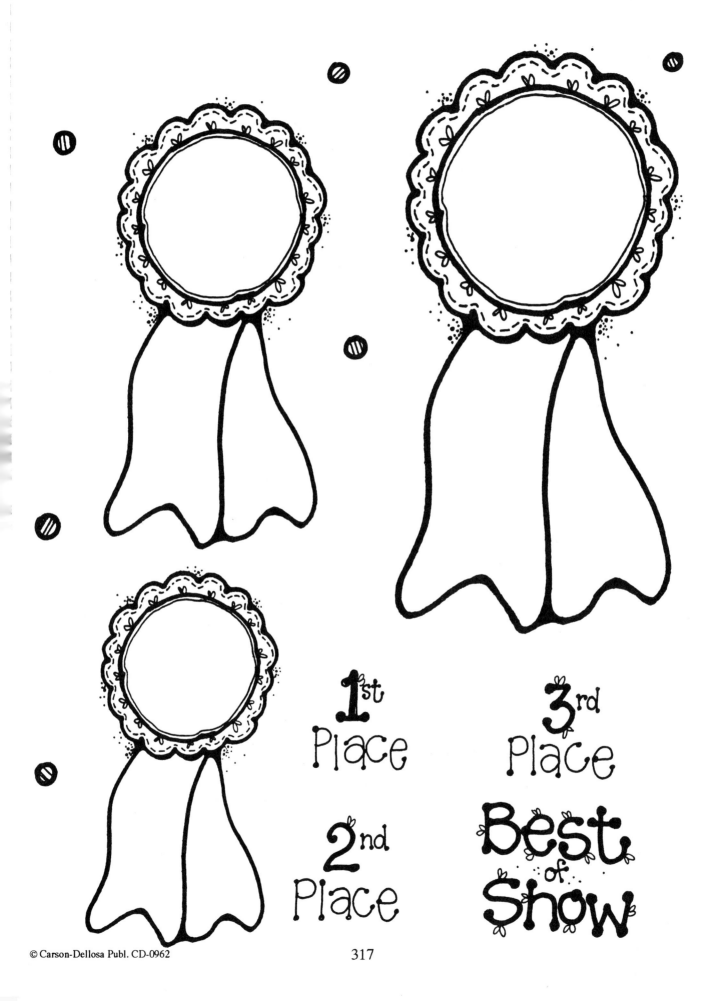

1st
Place

3rd
Place

2nd
Place

Best
of
Show

A Message to Parents

March

March March

April

April April

329

331

335

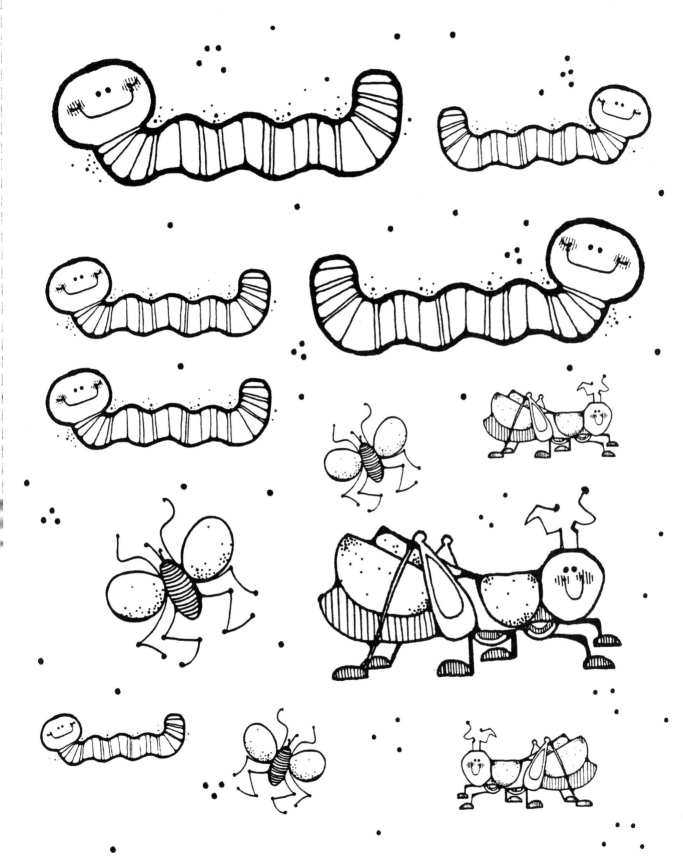

fold

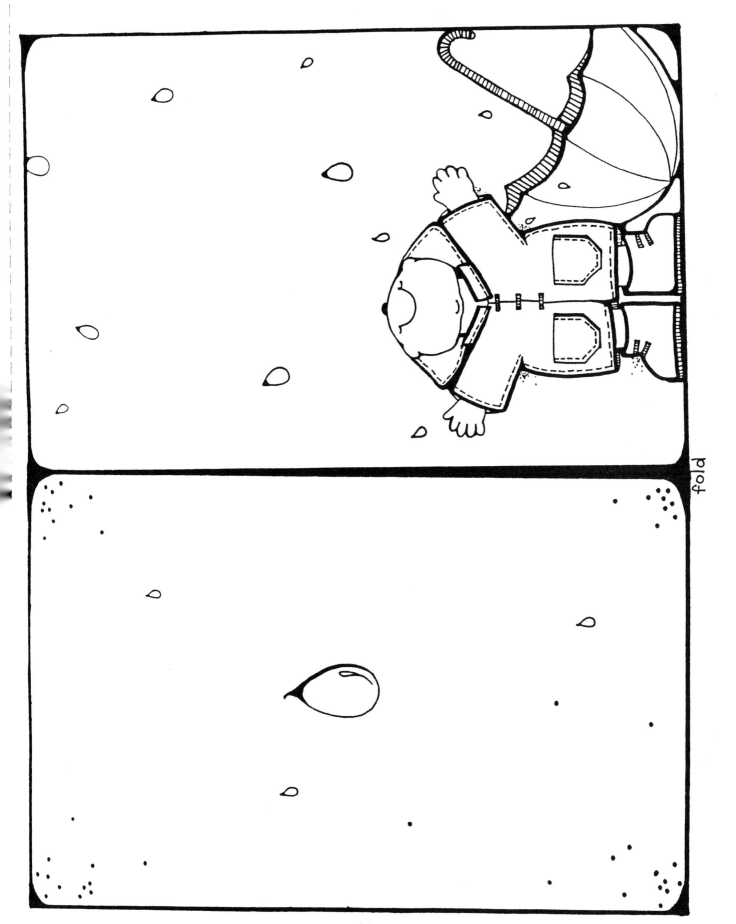

fold

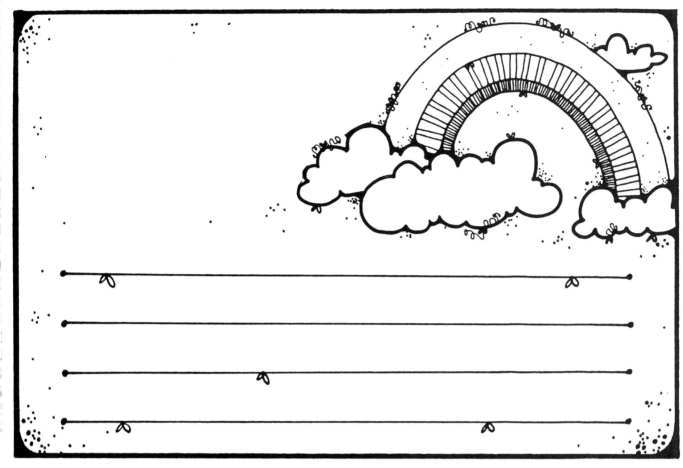

Happy Easter

from your teacher

fold

somebunny special!

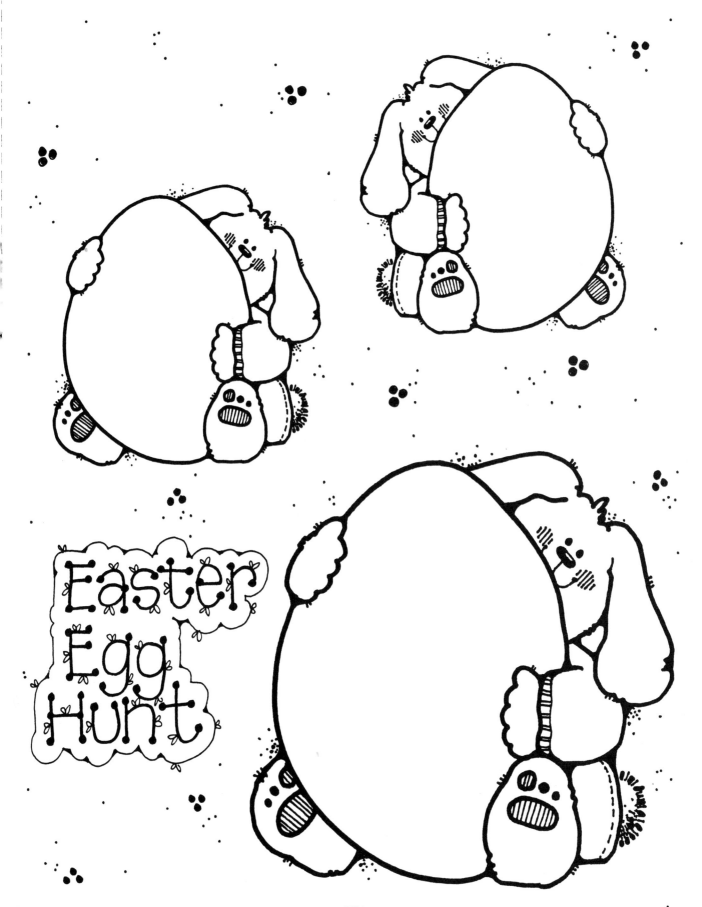

Easter Egg Hunt

To
From

Happy Easter
from your teacher

355

357

361

Happy Mother's Day

I ♥ MY MOM

I ♥ MY MOM

369

Father's Day

Father's Day

HELP!

We need the following for our class...

Thanks for your help!

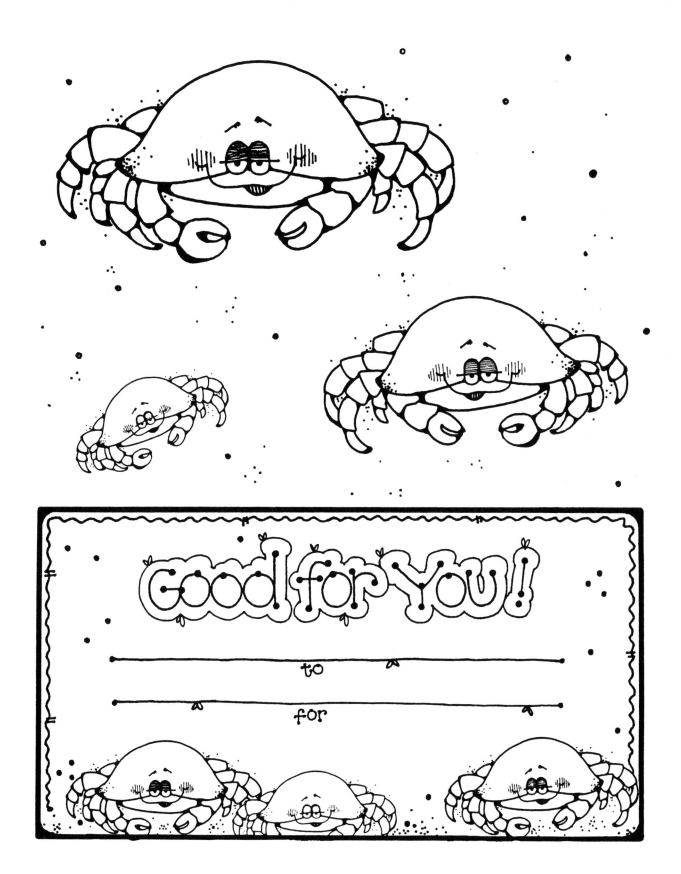

Good for YOU!

_____
to

_____
for

389

May

May

may

June

June

June

393

News to the Parents

A Note to Parents

401

403

SCHOOL'S OUT !!

407

I know my address

_____ name

_____ street

_____ city & state

_____ zip

411

SUMMER NEWS

415

SUMMER SCHOOL

How I spent my summer....

SUMMER VACATION!

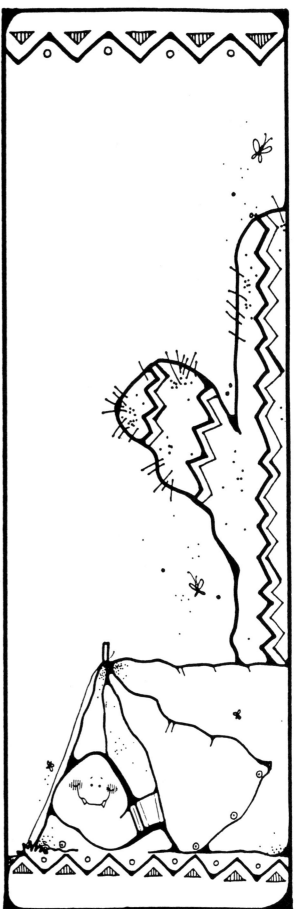

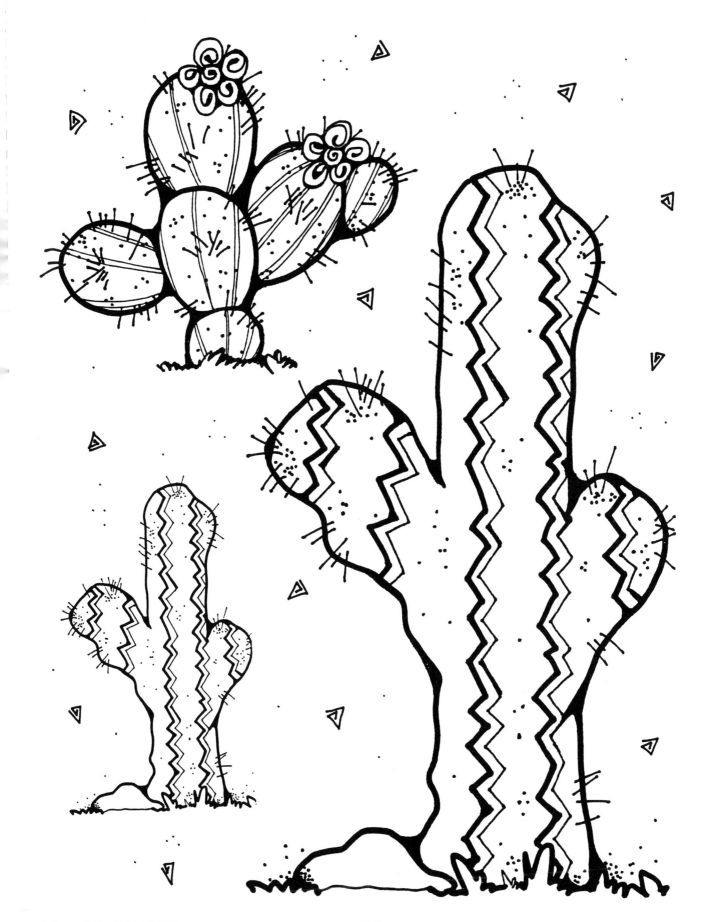

429

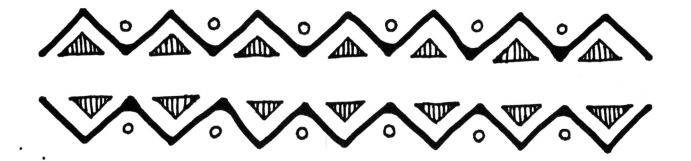

433

DAYCAMP NEWS

435

437

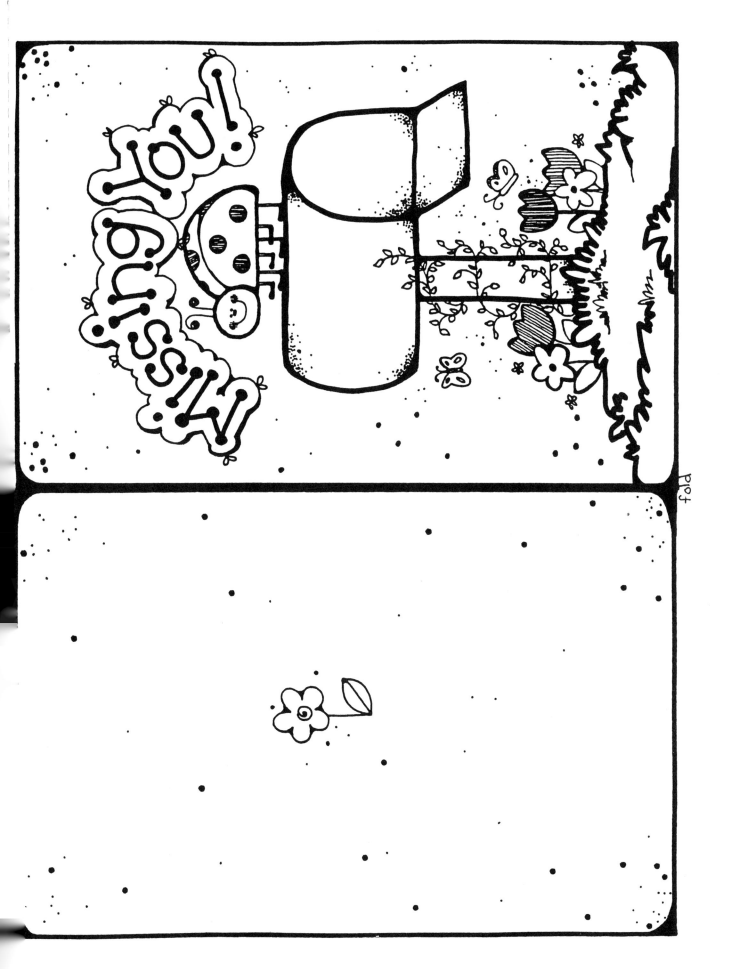

441

This book belongs to...

Summer Reading

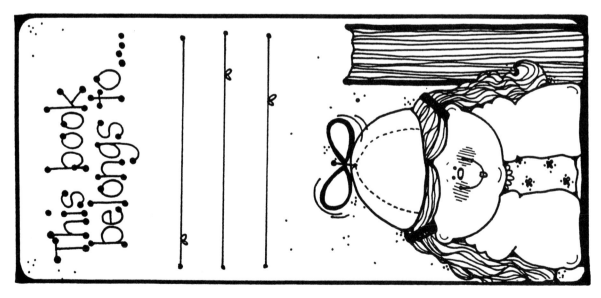

This book belongs to...

445

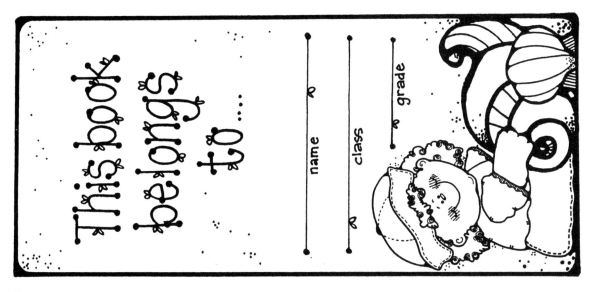

This book belongs to....

name

class

grade

Read It!

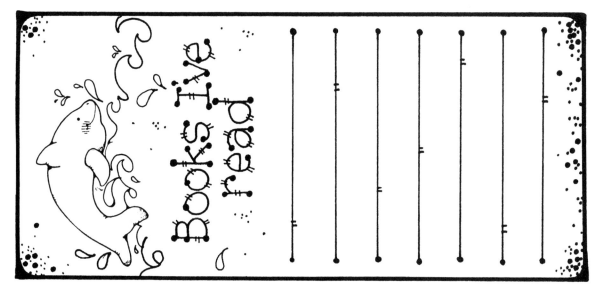

Books I've read

SUMMER PICNIC

SUMMER PICNIC

Be Sure to Come!

Be Sure to Come!

Nothing "BEETS" a great Volunteer !

Don't Forget...

SOCCER SCHEDULE

GOOD SPORT AWARD

_____ name

_____
date   teacher

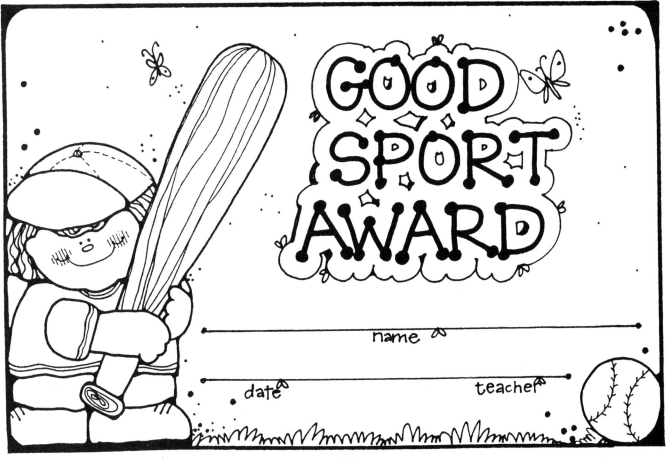

GOOD SPORT AWARD

_____ name

_____
date   teacher

Baseball Schedule

BUSY BEES!

Spelling

Graduation

this certifies that

_____

has successfully completed

_____

_____
date   teacher

Graduation

this certifies that

_____

has successfully completed

_____

_____
date   teacher

fold

congratulations

T.V Worth Watching...

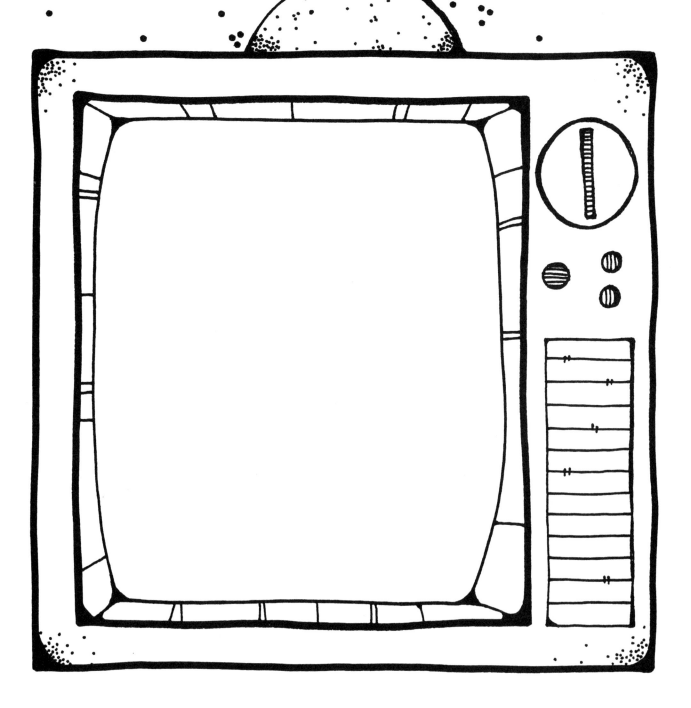